THE STORY OF THE
SECOND WORLD WAR
FOR CHILDREN
1939-1945

Executive Editor: Selina Wood
Project Art Editor: Russell Knowles
Design: Russell Knowles, David Ball
Illustrations: Peter Liddiard
Editorial: Paul Virr
Picture Research: Steve Behan
Production: Claire Hayward

This edition published in 2019 by Carlton Kids.
Text, design and illustration © 2010 by Carlton Books Limited
Published in 2010 by Carlton Books Limited
20 Mortimer Street
London W1T 3JW
10 9 8 7 6 5 4 3 2 1
A CIP catalogue record for this book is available from the British
Library.
ISBN: 978-1-78312-450-3
Printed in Hong Kong

IN PARTNERSHIP WITH

THE STORY OF THE
SECOND WORLD WAR
FOR CHILDREN
1939-1945

PETER CHRISP

CARLTON
KiDS

This is a map of the world in September 1942. It shows Allied and Axis countries, and territory under their control or influence. Major battles of the Second World War are also indicated.

MAP KEY

Allied

Axis

Area of Japanese control in the Pacific Ocean

Neutral countries

Major land battle

Major tank battle

Pacific sea battle

Atlantic sea battle

GREENLAND

ICELAND

BRITAIN
IRELAND   London

D-DAY

FRAN

BATTLE OF THE
ATLANTIC

CANADA

Ottawa

Washington, DC   New York

UNITED STATES
OF AMERICA
(USA)

ATLANTIC

OCEAN

SPAIN

PORTUGAL

FRENC
NORT
AFRIC

West Indies

FRENCH W
AFRICA

Dakar

VENEZUELA

COLOMBIA

ECUADOR

PERU   BRAZIL

BOLIVIA

CHILE
ARGENTINA

A WORLD AT WAR

World War II, from 1939 to 1945, was the biggest and deadliest conflict in history. Many countries took part, and fighting took place all across the world. More than 55 million people were killed, most of them civilians.

Unlike previous wars, which were mainly fought between armies on battlefields, World War II was a "people's war." Civilians were at the center of the action, as cities were devastated by aerial bombing. Workers on the "home front," making armaments and growing food, were as important to victory in the war as soldiers.

RIGHT: German and Italian tanks at El Alamein, in the North African desert.

LEFT: Finnish ski troops, fighting in the winter snow against the Soviets.

ABOVE: A Japanese cruiser in flames during the 1942 Battle of Midway, in the middle of the Pacific.

IN EVERY CLIMATE

The war was fought on land, at sea, in the air, and in every possible climate. Soldiers battled in the steamy jungles of Southeast Asia and in the winter snow of Russia. Great tank armies rolled through the North African desert. Across the wide Pacific Ocean, there were sea battles between the biggest naval forces in history. Beneath the Atlantic, German submarines, called U-boats, hunted convoys of merchant ships.

NEW WAYS OF FIGHTING

The war saw many new ways of fighting. Cities on each side were heavily bombed, in order to destroy people's will to fight. For the first time, invasions were carried out by air, by paratroopers. The development of the aircraft carrier—a warship that carries fighter aircraft—meant that air battles could be fought in the middle of the ocean. There were many new inventions, as scientists on each side raced to find war-winning weapons. Most deadly of all was the atomic bomb, a single bomb that could destroy a whole city in seconds.

LEFT: German paratroopers land in Crete, Greece, in May 1941, taking part in the first aerial invasion, or invasion from the air.

> **"The whole of the warring nations are engaged, not only soldiers, but the entire population. . . . The fronts are everywhere."**
>
> Winston Churchill, August 1940

ABOVE: The ruins of the city of Dresden, Germany, following two massive bombing raids in February 1945.

THE GATHERING STORM

There was a slow buildup to the outbreak of World War II. World War I, from 1914 to 1918, left Europe in ruins and up to 21 million dead. Afterward, the victors redrew the map of Europe, punishing the losing nations, Germany and Austria.

Under the Treaty of Versailles, written by Britain, France, and the United States in 1919, the Austrian Empire was dismantled. Germany lost territory to Poland and France and had to give up its large army. Blamed for starting the war, the Germans also had to pay huge sums of money to the winning nations.

Most Germans felt humiliated by the Treaty of Versailles. The treaty was opposed by a new political party called the National Socialist German Workers Party, or Nazi Party. Its leader, elected in 1921, was Adolf Hitler, an ex-soldier with a domineering personality who believed that Germany had been betrayed.

DENMARK

North Sea

Baltic Sea

Danzig

EAST PRUSSIA

• Hamburg

Berlin •

P O L A N D

Warsaw

NETHERLANDS

G E R M A N Y

River Rhine

BELGIUM

Frankfurt •

Prague •

CZECHOSLOVAKIA

F R A N C E

River Danube

Munich •

AUSTRIA

GERMANY, 1919

Germany before 1919

Parts of Germany lost after the Treaty of Versailles

HITLER'S RISE TO POWER

In 1929, there was a worldwide financial crisis, which led to soaring unemployment. In Germany, the government appeared to be unable to deal with the crisis. People wanted strong leadership, which Hitler promised to provide.

In the election of July 1932, the Nazis won the largest number of seats in the Reichstag, or Parliament. Hitler was appointed chancellor (head of government) in January 1933. He took on the title of Führer, meaning "leader."

ABOVE: In New York, women line up for food following the stock market crash of 1929.

BELOW: The Nazi message was that, under Hitler, there was "One People, One Reich (realm), One Führer."

13·MÄRZ 1938
EIN VOLK EIN REICH.
EIN FÜHRER

NAZIS AND FASCISTS

The Nazis had a lot in common with the Italian Fascists, whose leader, Benito Mussolini, had ruled Italy as a dictator since 1922. Hitler and Mussolini presented themselves as heroes who would make their countries great again, and they demanded total obedience. Members of both parties wore military-style uniforms and had special symbols and salutes. Mussolini and Hitler were political allies prior to and during World War II.

RIGHT: Like Hitler, Mussolini was a powerful speaker, who inspired loyalty and devotion in his followers.

STEPS TO WAR

BELOW: German police marching through Austria in 1938. Supporters of the Germans give the Nazi salute.

After making himself dictator of Germany in 1933, Adolf Hitler was in a position to break the Treaty of Versailles. Hitler guessed, correctly, that the British and French would do little to stop him.

Hitler's first move was to build up Germany's armed forces. At first he did this in secret. It was only in 1935, after the Luftwaffe, or air force, had 2,500 planes and the army had 300,000 soldiers, that he revealed that Germany was rearming. He then sent troops into the Rhineland, a part of Germany that was supposed to be free of military forces. This was a threat to France, but France did not react. Then, in 1938, the German army marched into Austria, and the two German-speaking nations were united.

LEFT: The symbol of the Nazi party was the swastika—a cross with arms bent at right angles. Red, black, and white were colours of the old German empire.

MUNICH CONFERENCE

Hitler then threatened neighboring Czechoslovakia. He demanded control over the Sudetenland, a Czech region with a population of more than three million German speakers. In September 1938, Chamberlain and Daladier, the British and French leaders, held a conference with Mussolini and Hitler in Munich. They agreed to make Czechoslovakia surrender the Sudetenland to the Germans. In return, Hitler promised that this would be his final demand.

BELOW: Nazi supporters pull down frontier signs between Germany and Czechoslovakia. With the German occupation, Czechoslovakia ceased to exist.

CZECHOSLOVAKIA, 1939

- Czechoslovakia in 1937
- Parts of Czechoslovakia occupied by Germany

GERMANY · Dresden · River Oder · Breslau
SUDETENLAND · Prague · River Elbe · BOHEMIA · Cracow · POLAND
MORAVIA · Brno
SUDETENLAND · SLOVAKIA · Kassa
RUTHENIA Occupied by Hungary
River Danube · Vienna · Bratislava
Salzburg
AUSTRIA · Budapest · ROMANIA
Graz · HUNGARY

APPEASEMENT

The British prime minister, Neville Chamberlain, felt that Germany had been unfairly treated by the Treaty of Versailles and that some of Hitler's actions were justified. So he followed a policy called appeasement—giving in to Hitler's demands in the hope of avoiding war. Hitler repeatedly lied to Chamberlain, claiming that each of his demands was the final one.

BELOW: On his return from the Munich Conference, Neville Chamberlain shows the public his signed agreement with Hitler.

THREATS TO POLAND

In March 1939, Hitler broke the promise made at Munich, and took over the rest of Czechoslovakia. Next he began to threaten Poland, demanding the return of the city of Danzig and the "Polish corridor" dividing Germany and East Prussia. At last, Chamberlain and Daladier decided to resist him. They warned Hitler that if he attacked Poland, they would declare war on Germany. Hitler, however, who had seen them back down in the past, did not believe that they really intended to fight.

ABOVE: A steel helmet belonging to a soldier in the German army.

BLITZKRIEG ON POLAND

On September 1, 1939, Adolf Hitler launched a surprise attack on Poland. Following bombing raids on Polish airfields, German tanks and armed vehicles swept over the borders, invading from the north, west, and south.

This was a new type of warfare, called blitzkrieg, or "lightning war." Its main features were surprise and speed. The Germans attacked without even declaring war on Poland. By attacking small sections of the Polish defenses, they concentrated their forces, allowing them to break through and then sweep behind enemy lines. The Poles faced the task of defending a 1,750-mile-long border. They had an army of 800,000 men, but it was poorly equipped, with 11 brigades of horse-mounted troops and only a few tanks.

LEFT: Polish cavalrymen fought bravely, but they had little chance against German tanks.

INVASION OF POLAND
September 1939

Baltic Sea · Königsberg · LITHUANIA · Danzig · EAST PRUSSIA · Chelmo · Bialystok · River Vistula · Warsaw · Berlin · Poznan · P O L A N D · Lodz · Chelm · Dresden · River Oder · River Bug · Prague · Cracow · Lwów · BOHEMIA · SLOVAKIA · G E R M A N Y · S O V I E T U N I O N

BELOW: By dive-bombing, a Stuka could hit targets such as bridges or troop columns with great accuracy.

RIGHT: German tanks sweep across the Polish plains. In the dry summer of 1939, this was perfect terrain for tanks.

SHOCK WEAPONS

One aim of blitzkrieg was to shock enemy troops, destroying their ability to fight back. The German Ju 87 Stuka dive-bomber, fitted with a screeching siren, was designed to cause terror as well as destruction. Armed with two machine guns and carrying five bombs, it plunged out of the sky at a steep angle and at great speed.

> "Poland will never rise again in the form of the Versailles Treaty."
>
> Adolf Hitler, September 19, 1939

THE WAR WIDENS

Two days after the invasion, Britain and France honored their guarantee to the Poles and declared war on Germany. Yet they were stunned by the speed of the German invasion. The final blow came on September 17, when the Soviet Union invaded Poland from the east. Joseph Stalin, the Soviet leader, had made a secret agreement with Hitler to divide Poland between them.

INSIDE A STUKA

WIRELESS

REAR GUNNER

PILOT'S SEAT

FUEL TANK

ENGINE

SIREN FOR DIVE-BOMBING

BOMB

HOME FRONT: BRITAIN

Air Raid Wardens WANTED

CIVIL DEFENCE

...ARE WANTED

NOW

GET IN... WITH YOUR LOCAL COU...

At the outbreak of war, it was expected that British cities would be heavily bombed by the Germans. To meet the threat, the government organized Air Raid Precautions (ARP). Gas masks were distributed in case of gas attacks, cities were blacked out, and children were evacuated to the country.

It was feared that in the event of bombing, there would be a panic flight from the cities. The government decided to evacuate, or withdraw, young children and mothers with babies from threatened areas. Evacuees, accompanied by teachers, were sent by train to the countryside, where host families took them in. This was a shock for the evacuees, most of whom had never seen the countryside. Their country hosts were equally shocked by the newcomers, who sometimes came from very poor urban areas. When the expected air raids did not come, many parents brought their children back to the cities.

RIGHT: The government called on members of the public to serve as air raid wardens. Around 1.5 million men and women volunteered for ARP duties.

ABOVE: A young girl evacuee, with her doll and luggage, waits nervously to be chosen by a host family.

ABOVE: An air raid warden gives directions to a family wearing gas masks during a practice drill for an air raid.

AIR RAID PRECAUTION WARDENS

ARP wardens enforced blackouts. A blackout's purpose was to stop bomber planes from finding cities at night. Street lights were put out, and people drew thick black curtains across their windows. Wardens patrolled the streets, shouting, "Put that light out!" In the event of a raid, sirens sounded the alarm and wardens guided people to shelters. They also distributed gas masks in case the Germans dropped bombs releasing poisonous gas.

RATIONING

Britain imported most of its food from overseas, using supply routes now threatened by German submarines. To ensure everyone got a fair share and to prevent people from hoarding food, on January 8, 1940, the government introduced rationing. Every person received a ration book, containing coupons to be handed to a shopkeeper when buying goods. Food, fuel, coal, and clothing were all rationed.

RIGHT: People were encouraged to grow vegetables such as carrots in their gardens.

DOCTOR CARROT the Children's best friend

RIGHT: The British royal family was issued with ration books to show that nobody had special privileges.

LEFT: Meat was in short supply. This tin of broth was brought across the Atlantic from Uruguay.

LEFT: Powdered egg was widely used during the war.

HOME-FRONT FOOD

DIG FOR VICTORY!

The British government realized that if the war continued for more than a few months, food supplies would soon run out.

"Dig for Victory" was a campaign started by the Ministry of Agriculture to encourage people to grow food in their gardens as a way of helping the war effort. All around the country, public gardens, flower beds, and sports fields were dug up and turned into vegetable plots.

People were also urged to keep chickens and ducks for eggs. Even scraps from the kitchen were saved to be fed to pigs.

DIG FOR VICTORY

ABOVE: Millions of "Dig for Victory" posters and leaflets were distributed to the public.

WOMEN'S LAND ARMY

Over 80,000 women volunteered to become "Land Girls," members of the Women's Land Army, set up to replace male farm workers who had joined the armed forces. Wearing brown and green uniforms, they drove tractors, milked cows, dug potatoes, and worked in sawmills.

BELOW: Members of the Women's Land Army preparing the soil to plant radishes.

FALL OF FRANCE

ABOVE: The Dutch surrendered after Rotterdam, their largest industrial city and port, was heavily bombed in May.

Following the conquest of Poland, there was little fighting for several months. This period, nicknamed the "Phony War," ended when Germany invaded Norway and Denmark. Then, on May 10, 1940, Hitler launched a new blitzkrieg against the Netherlands, Belgium, and France.

The campaign began with an airborne attack on the Netherlands and Belgium, where 4,000 German parachutists seized bridges and airfields. Motorized divisions then swept over the borders. The British and French advanced into Belgium to meet the invasion, not realizing that they had walked into a trap. The main German forces were farther south, where they broke through French lines in the Ardennes. This wooded region was wrongly thought to be unsuitable for tanks and was thinly defended. Once they had made the breakthrough, the German tanks raced north toward the English Channel, encircling the British and French armies.

INVASION OF FRANCE May 1940

ABOVE: Defeated French infantrymen surrender to the Germans.

RETREAT TO DUNKIRK

Though the British and French—known as the Allies—had more soldiers and tanks than the Germans, they were overwhelmed by the blitzkrieg tactics. They retreated north toward the English Channel, under constant attack from Stuka dive-bombers.

On May 20, the Germans reached the coast before the Allies got there. In a surprise move, Hitler ordered the German advance to halt for three days. This allowed the British to rescue 338,226 soldiers from the beaches of Dunkirk, though they left all their tanks and artillery behind.

ABOVE: British, French, and Belgian soldiers are evacuated from Dunkirk, France. All kinds of seagoing craft were used in the rescue, which lasted nine days.

FRENCH SURRENDER

On June 10, the Italian dictator, Mussolini, also declared war on France and invaded from the south. Meanwhile, the German army was advancing southwest toward the French capital, Paris, which it occupied on June 14.

Three days later, French leaders asked for an end to the fighting. After visiting Paris on June 23, Hitler said, "That was the greatest and finest moment of my life."

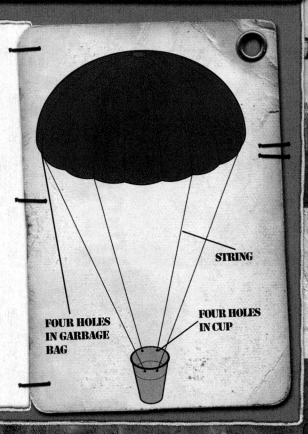

RIGHT: Though the French had antitank mines, they had not placed them in the Ardennes, where the German army broke through.

ABOVE: On June 23, Hitler took a sightseeing trip to Paris, the city he had conquered.

HOW TO MAKE A PARACHUTE

You can make your own simple parachute using common household items:

STEP 1
Cut out a square about 1 foot wide from a garbage bag.

STEP 2
Make four holes an equal distance apart around the edge of a plastic cup. Make a hole in each corner of your garbage bag.

STEP 3
Cut four pieces of string, each about 1.5 feet long.

STEP 4
Tie one end of one of a string to a hole in the cup and the other end to a hole in the parachute. Repeat three times.

Now add a plastic soldier to the cup and try it out!

STRING

FOUR HOLES IN GARBAGE BAG

FOUR HOLES IN CUP

BATTLE OF BRITAIN

Throughout the hot summer of 1940, Spitfire and Hurricane fighter planes fought a desperate battle against the Luftwaffe (German air force) in the skies over southern England. The campaign became known as the Battle of Britain.

ABOVE: A badge worn by one of 88 Czech pilots who joined the RAF and fought in the battle.

After the Dunkirk disaster, Hitler expected Britain to make peace. But Prime Minister Winston Churchill's determination to fight on forced Hitler to plan a seaborne invasion, called Operation Sea Lion. For an invasion to succeed, the Germans needed to control the air over the English Channel. Hermann Göring, the Luftwaffe chief, promised Hitler that he would sweep the Royal Air Force (RAF) from the skies. Starting on July 10, 1940, he sent large formations of bomber and fighter planes to attack the RAF.

CHURCHILL

Throughout the 1930s, Winston Churchill (1874–1965) was a leading opponent of appeasement, warning of the dangers posed by Hitler. Proven right by the outbreak of the war, he was chosen to lead an all-party government in May 1940. As Prime Minister, Churchill stiffened British determination to resist Hitler with stirring speeches to the British nation.

BELOW: Shoulder badges worn by fighter pilots from Commonwealth countries.

NEW ZEALAND

CANADA

RHODESIA

LEFT: RAF fighter pilots scramble for their planes. Their average age was 19.

LEFT: Hurricanes destroyed more German aircraft than any other Allied fighter plane.

RIGHT: The Messerschmitt Bf 109 was armed with two machine guns and two cannons, carried under the wings.

DOGFIGHTS

Much of the fighting took the form of single combat between German Messerschmitt Bf 109 fighter planes and Hurricanes and Spitfires. Such combats were nicknamed "dogfights." Survival depended on the flying skill and split-second reactions of the pilots. Flying daily missions was exhausting and by September the RAF was close to a breaking point. Yet Göring had been unable to win control of the air and, on September 17, Hitler postponed the invasion.

SPITFIRE

In 1940, the Supermarine Spitfire was the fastest and most maneuverable fighter plane. It could reach 367 mph, compared to the 342 mph of the Messerschmitt Bf 109. One drawback was that its large fuel supply meant that if it was hit, it often burst into flames.

RIGHT: A radar tower based in Hampshire, England. There was a series of radar stations across the south of England.

RADAR

Britain's secret weapon in the summer of 1940 was radiolocation, later called radar. This was based on a chain of coastal stations that transmitted radio waves to detect enemy planes. Göring did not realize just how effective these stations were, and made little attempt to destroy them. Thanks to radar, the RAF knew in advance where the German bomber and fighter planes were heading before they even reached the coast of Britain.

THE BLITZ

In September 1940, the Luftwaffe gave up fighting the RAF in the daytime and began to bomb London and other British cities by night. The new campaign, called the Blitz, lasted eight months and resulted in the deaths of 43,000 civilians.

The Blitz was started by Hitler as vengeance for British air raids on the German capital, Berlin. By hitting cities, Hitler hoped to destroy the will of Britain to fight on. Another motive was to hit war factories, which were based in the cities. The campaign began on September 7, when 247 German bombers attacked London's East End, setting the docks on fire. It was the first of 57 successive night raids on London.

BELOW: A wrecked bus in the ruins of the city of Coventry, England, following a massive raid in November 1940.

LEFT: A Heinkel 111 bomber plane flying over London. Marked by a U-shaped bend in the River Thames, the East End was easy to spot from the air.

EWK 240

SHELTERING

The British government built street shelters, made of brick and concrete, that could hold up to 50 people. Many Londoners, however, felt safer in underground train stations. They camped on the platforms and beside the rails. At first, the authorities tried to discourage this, afraid that people would start to live underground. Eventually they gave in, and some stations were actually closed to trains and converted into shelters.

ABOVE: Aldwych tube station in London, used as a shelter from bombs, in October 1940.

ABOVE: Members of the Auxiliary Fire Service fighting fires in the ruins after a raid. All volunteers, they worked tirelessly.

COVENTRY

Starting in November 1940, the Luftwaffe began to bomb cities in the industrial Midlands. On November 14, Coventry, with its 21 aircraft and tank factories, was hit by the biggest raid of the whole Blitz. During a ten-hour raid, 515 bombers dropped hundreds of tons of bombs on the city. As fire swept through Coventry, more than 60,000 buildings were destroyed. Around 600 people died. Despite the destruction, war production was back to normal within six weeks.

ANDERSON SHELTER

More than two million British homes had an Anderson Shelter, first issued by the government in February 1939. Made of corrugated steel panels, it was half buried in a yard and then covered with soil. Without drainage, it often flooded with rainwater.

RIGHT: Neighbors put up Anderson shelters in their backyards.

21

OPERATION BARBAROSSA

In June 1941, with Britain still undefeated, Hitler widened the war and attacked the Soviet Union. The invasion, named Operation Barbarossa, was to be a new blitzkrieg. Hitler expected to conquer the Soviet Union within weeks.

Hitler's long-term aim had always been to seize "living space" for the German people in eastern Europe. He also believed that the Soviet Red Army would be easy to defeat. The invasion, launched on June 22, came as a complete surprise to the Soviets. The Germans advanced rapidly toward the important industrial city of Leningrad, in the north, and Moscow, the capital, farther south.

By September, they had captured 700,000 Soviet prisoners and surrounded Leningrad. Yet although the Red Army suffered major losses, it was continually reinforced. Soviet tank and plane factories were moved east, well out of range of German bombers.

BELOW: A Russian infantry cap badge.

BELOW: German tanks and armored vehicles crossing the vast plains of Russia in July 1941.

INVASION OF SOVIET UNION
June 1941

SWEDEN
Leningrad
Riga
Baltic Sea
Moscow
Smolensk
Minsk
Berlin
Tambov
GERMAN REICH
SOVIET UNION
UKRAINE
Kursk
River Don
Prague
Lvov
Kiev
River Volga
Vienna
SLOVAKIA
River Dnieper
Stalingrad
HUNGARY
Odessa
Rostov-on-Don
ROMANIA
YUGOSLAVIA

RIGHT: German troops bombard Leningrad with artillery. Soviet figures claim that 150,000 shells were fired at the city.

LEFT: Russian women dig defenses in Leningrad in October 1941.

LENINGRAD AND MOSCOW

The Germans reached Leningrad in September, beginning a siege that would last almost 900 days, leading to the deaths of over one million Soviet citizens. Farther south, the advance on Moscow was slowed by heavy autumn rains, which turned primitive Russian roads into flowing mud. Soon, a bitter Russian winter set in. With frozen fuel, the tanks could no longer move. The Germans had not prepared for winter fighting. The soldiers were still wearing summer uniforms, which they stuffed with newspapers in an attempt to keep warm.

LEFT: Two Nazis try to clear a path for their car, stuck in the thick mud on a Russian road during heavy rains.

BELOW: A German soldier looking weather-beaten in the Russian winter.

SOVIET COUNTERATTACK

Meanwhile, Stalin had been reinforcing the army in Moscow with fresh troops from Siberia, who were trained to fight in winter. In December, the Red Army was strong enough to launch its counterattack. This caused a crisis in the German leadership. When Hitler's generals asked him for permission to retreat, he refused, saying, "Is it any less cold fifty miles back?" Losing faith in the senior generals, Hitler now made himself direct commander-in-chief of the army. Despite huge losses, the Germans managed to beat back the Soviet attacks and hold on to their defensive positions throughout the winter.

RUSSIAN WINTER SURVIVAL

The war in the Soviet Union was sometimes fought in temperatures colder than -31°F. Survival in these conditions depends on:

- Adequate warm clothing
- Enough food—extra calories keep you warm
- Shelter from chilling winds and blizzards
- Proper medical treatment for conditions such as frostbite

64°F

32°F

0°F

-31°F

1939–1945

BATTLE OF THE ATLANTIC

From bases on the French Atlantic coast, German submarines, called U-boats, launched a deadly campaign against Allied merchant ships bringing food, oil, and vital supplies across the Atlantic from the United States.

For protection, merchant ships set off in great convoys of up to 60 vessels, sailing in a dozen or more columns. On the outsides, fast naval warships, called destroyers and corvettes, hunted for U-boats. They used sonar—sound waves that bounced back when they hit a submarine. Once they found a U-boat, they dropped depth charges. These bombs exploded underwater and could sink a U-boat, or disable it, forcing it to the surface.

BELOW: Allied merchant ships sailing in a convoy across the North Atlantic.

RIGHT: The crew of a US naval vessel watch as the depth charge they have dropped explodes.

> **"The only thing that really frightened me during the war was the U-boat peril."**
>
> Winston Churchill, *The Second World War*, Volume II

WOLF PACKS

Starting in October 1940, U-boats attacked the convoys in large groups called wolf packs. They waited until night, when they could surface without being seen. U-boats were faster on the surface than they were underwater and could quickly maneuver into position for an attack. A wolf pack might follow a convoy for several nights, making repeated attacks with torpedoes. Each sailor dreaded nightfall, wondering if his ship would survive until dawn. During the Battle of the Atlantic, U-boats sank 2,603 ships. Over 30,000 British and Allied sailors lost their lives in the cold sea.

U-BOAT SET-BACKS

The Allies found new ways to fight the wolf packs. They developed long-range bomber planes, and a radio detection system to track U-boats by their broadcasts. In the spring of 1943, so many U-boats were sunk that the wolf pack tactics had to be abandoned. They had suffered worse casualty rates than any other service: out of 40,900 U-boat crewmen, 28,000 died in their submarines.

ABOVE: Using his periscope, the U-boat captain scans the surface for ships to attack.

RIGHT: In the cramped forward compartment, the crew took turns sleeping in the few bunks.

LIVING CONDITIONS

A U-boat was cramped, hot, and stuffy, with a constant smell of engine oil. The crew of around 50 men shared a single toilet. To save water, they gave up washing and shaving. The men lived on tinned food that, according to one commander, "tasted of U-boat; that is, diesel oil with a flavor of mold." Yet the crew had a strong sense of comradeship, united by the dangers they shared.

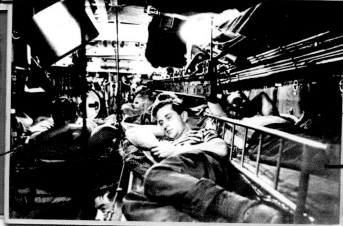

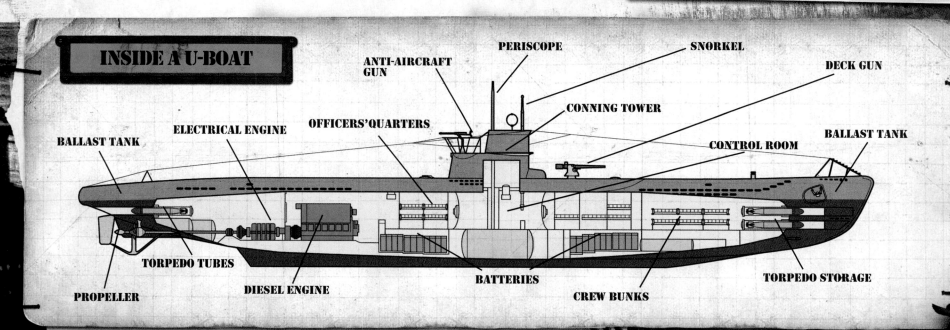

INSIDE A U-BOAT

ANTI-AIRCRAFT GUN

PERISCOPE

SNORKEL

DECK GUN

CONNING TOWER

OFFICERS' QUARTERS

CONTROL ROOM

BALLAST TANK

ELECTRICAL ENGINE

BALLAST TANK

TORPEDO TUBES

TORPEDO STORAGE

PROPELLER

DIESEL ENGINE

BATTERIES

CREW BUNKS

DESERT WAR

Between 1940 and 1943, a narrow strip of the North African coast changed hands five times, as Allied and Axis tank armies fought across the desert sands.

For Germany and Italy—now known as the Axis powers—the purpose of the desert war was to conquer Egypt, occupied by a British and Commonwealth army. If Egypt fell, Hitler could seize the Arabian oil fields and cut off Britain's supply route through the Suez Canal.

The campaign began in the summer of 1940, when Mussolini's Italian army invaded Egypt. Although outnumbered, the British used blitzkrieg tactics learned from the Germans to break through the Italian lines. British tanks swept 500 miles into Libya, capturing 130,000 prisoners. To prevent total defeat, Hitler sent General Erwin Rommel and a German tank force to Africa in February 1941. Rommel's army was called the Afrika Korps.

BELOW: Rommel's men were proud to belong to the Afrika Korps. They wore this cuff title on their sleeves.

AFRIKAKORPS

THE DESERT FOX

Erwin Rommel (1891–1944), commander of the Afrika Korps, was the most famous German general of World War II. During his first desert offensive, in March 1941, he advanced with a force including dummy tanks, built from wood and mounted on Volkswagen cars, and ordered his men to stir up dust clouds. Convinced his army was bigger than it was, the British retreated. Such cunning tactics won Rommel the nickname the "Desert Fox."

BELOW: The German air force in Libya during 1941. Junkers aircraft were the backbone of Rommel's supply system to his forces.

LEFT: Afrika Korps troops fire an 88mm gun, the standard German antiaircraft and antitank weapon of the war.

BACK AND FORTH

As an army advanced across the desert, it grew weaker, due to lengthening supply lines and tanks worn out by desert sand. Meanwhile, a retreating army concentrated its forces until it was strong enough to counterattack. Final victory depended on the ability of each side to send in reinforcements and fuel. Here, the Allies had a great advantage.

EL ALAMEIN

The greatest desert battle was fought at El Alamein in October 1942. The Afrika Korps faced the British 8th Army, commanded by General Bernard Montgomery. Unlike Rommel, Montgomery was cautious, only attacking when he was certain of victory. He launched his offensive with twice as many tanks as Rommel, including 300 new US-built Sherman tanks. Rommel was beaten in the first large-scale British land victory of the war. Montgomery advanced through Libya and Tunisia, while Allied forces landed in Morocco and Algeria. The Afrika Korps finally surrendered in May 1943.

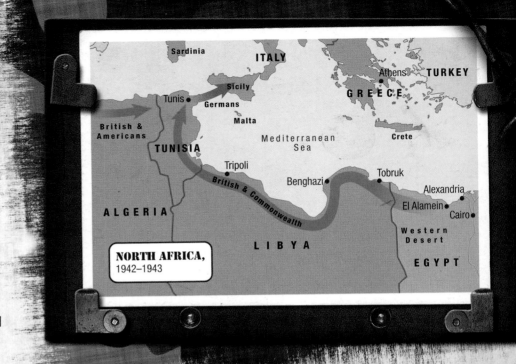

NORTH AFRICA,
1942–1943

"We have a very daring and skillful opponent against us. And may I say across the havoc of war, a great general..."
Winston Churchill on Rommel, 1942

BELOW: Soldiers of the 8th Army capture a German tank.

SUNDAY DECEMBER 7 1941

PEARL HARBOR

On December 7, 1941, the US Pacific Fleet at Pearl Harbor was hit by a surprise attack from Japanese bomber and fighter planes. With this shock event the war became a truly global conflict.

The Japanese had been building an empire in Asia since 1931, when they invaded Manchuria, followed by China in 1937. After the fall of France to Germany in 1940, Japan occupied northern French Indochina.

US President Roosevelt demanded that Japan give up these conquests. In July 1941, he cut off their supply of oil, which was mostly imported from the United States. Faced with this threat to their plans for conquest, Japan decided to go to war with America. Since the United States was a more powerful nation, Japan's only hope lay in a surprise attack on the US fleet.

EMPEROR HIROHITO

To the Japanese people, Emperor Hirohito (ruled 1926–1989) was a godlike descendant of the sun goddess. Belief in the divine status of their emperor made the Japanese feel superior to all other nations. Yet Hirohito did not directly rule Japan. Real power was held by the military, headed after October 1941 by General Hideki Tojo, who claimed to rule on the emperor's behalf.

ABOVE: The battleship USS *West Virginia* in flames, after being hit by up to nine Japanese planes at Pearl Harbor.

ATTACK ON PEARL HARBOR

The Pearl Harbor attack was planned and led by Admiral Isoroku Yamamoto. During the night of December 6–7, he secretly took a fleet of six aircraft carriers 275 miles north of Pearl Harbor. Before sunrise, over 350 bomber, torpedo, and fighter planes took off from the carriers.

They reached their target undetected, finding US fighter planes on the ground, where they destroyed 188 of them. Facing little resistance, the Japanese sank or badly damaged 18 ships and killed 2,335 US servicemen. Yet the destruction could have been worse. Three US carriers escaped the attack, since they were at sea.

RIGHT: The front page of the *New York Daily News* carried the shocking story of the Japanese attack.

BELOW: After USS *Shaw* was hit by three bombs, fire spread through the destroyer, causing a massive explosion when it reached the ammunition stores.

ROOSEVELT

Franklin Delano Roosevelt (1882–1945), the only US president to be elected more than twice, served during four terms from 1933 to 1945. He stood up to Nazi and Japanese aggression, sending military aid to the Chinese fighting Japan and to Britain, France, and the Soviet Union. However, he knew that most Americans did not want to fight a foreign war. Everything changed after the Pearl Harbor attack, which united the nation against the Japanese.

JAPANESE TRIUMPHS

The attack on Pearl Harbor was part of a bigger plan to create a vast Asian empire. On the same day as the raid, the Japanese invaded the Philippines, where US army and navy forces were based, and the British-held Hong Kong and Malaya. They carried out a lightning attack before the Americans and British could react. Everywhere, the Japanese were victorious. On December 11, Adolf Hitler also declared war on the United States. It was now truly a world war.

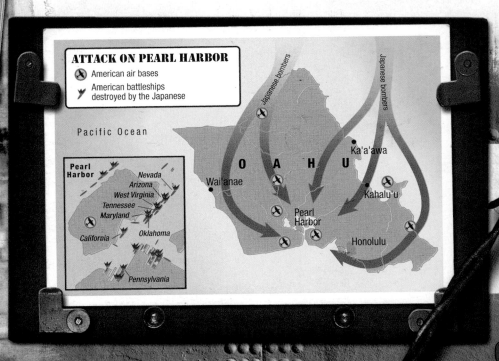

ATTACK ON PEARL HARBOR

✈ American air bases

↙ American battleships destroyed by the Japanese

Pacific Ocean

Pearl Harbor

Nevada
Arizona
West Virginia
Tennessee
Maryland
California
Oklahoma
Pennsylvania

O A H U

Wai'anae

Ka'a'awa

Kahalu'u

Pearl Harbor

Honolulu

BATTLE OF MIDWAY

BELOW: Burning oil tanks belch out smoke at Midway after the Japanese attack. In the foreground, three albatross chicks remain unharmed.

In May 1942, a vast fleet set sail from Japan for the island of Midway, in the middle of the Pacific Ocean. Admiral Yamamoto, commanding the fleet, planned to finish off the US Navy in the Pacific.

Yamamoto hoped that invading Midway, a US territory, would draw the US Pacific Fleet to defend the island. In particular, he wanted to sink the three American aircraft carriers that had escaped his attack on Pearl Harbor.

He was confident of victory because his fleet, which included eight aircraft carriers with 500 planes, was much larger than the US force. Once Midway was captured, the Japanese believed they could threaten the west coast of the United States and force the Americans to make peace.

YAMAMOTO

Admiral Isoroku Yamamto (1884–1943), commander of the Japanese Combined Fleet, was a brilliant mastermind who planned the attacks on Pearl Harbor and Midway. On April 18, 1943, his plane was shot down by 16 US fighters, acting on secret intelligence. His successor, Admiral Kaga, said, "There was only one Yamamoto and no one can replace him."

"There is such a beautiful moon tonight. Shall we watch it as we sink?"

Admiral Tamon Yamaguchi, on a sinking Japanese carrier

WAITING FOR THE ATTACK

Although outnumbered, the Americans, commanded by Admiral Chester Nimitz, had three advantages. The island of Midway gave their planes somewhere to land, even if the enemy sank their carriers. Unlike the Japanese, they had radar to find the enemy fleet. Most importantly, they had broken the code used by the Japanese for radio messages, so Nimitz knew that the attack was coming. It would not be another Pearl Harbor.

LEFT: Two US Navy dive-bombers in action. Below the aircraft, a long column of smoke rises from a burning Japanese ship.

LEFT: Crewmen on the deck of USS *Yorktown*. The carrier is tipping over after being hit by three Japanese bombs and two torpedoes.

SINKING THE CARRIERS

By luck, the fourth wave of US bombers reached the carriers when many Japanese planes were on deck refueling. This gave them a clear shot at their targets. Soon three carriers were sinking. Planes from a fourth carrier successfully attacked the US carrier *Yorktown*, but then it too was sunk. With nowhere to land, the Japanese planes had to crash into the sea. In the end, the Japanese lost 292 planes along with their best pilots. Japan had suffered a disastrous defeat.

LEFT: The *Mikuma*, a Japanese heavy cruiser, in flames after being hit by US dive-bombers. Shortly after, the ship rolled over and sank.

THE BATTLE BEGINS

In the early hours of June 4, 108 Japanese bomber planes reached Midway, where they bombed the airfields. The US fighter planes were outnumbered and no match for the Japanese. Meanwhile, Nimitz's land-based bombers attacked the Japanese carriers, but all of them missed their targets. Then the US carrier force north of Midway joined the battle, sending four waves of planes to attack the Japanese carriers. The first three waves were beaten off and it looked like the Japanese would win the battle.

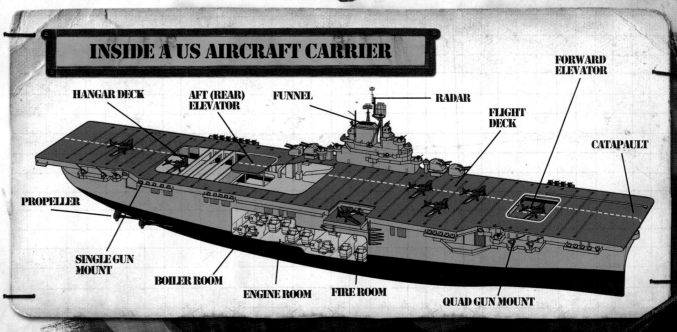

INSIDE A US AIRCRAFT CARRIER

HANGAR DECK

AFT (REAR) ELEVATOR

FUNNEL

RADAR

FORWARD ELEVATOR

FLIGHT DECK

CATAPULT

PROPELLER

SINGLE GUN MOUNT

BOILER ROOM

ENGINE ROOM

FIRE ROOM

QUAD GUN MOUNT

STALINGRAD

The battle for the Soviet city of Stalingrad, from August 1942 until February 1943, saw the hardest fighting of the war. Each side viewed the capture of the city as the key to victory or defeat.

In the summer of 1942, Hitler launched a new offensive. Its aim was to seize the oil fields of the Caucasus Mountains in the southern Soviet Union. If successful, the Germans would cut off the Red Army's oil supply and find the fuel they desperately needed for their own tanks and planes.

By August, the German 6th Army had reached the great industrial city of Stalingrad, a major port on the River Volga. The Soviet 62nd Army defending the city was less well armed than the German attacking force. But Stalin was determined that the city named after him should be held at all costs. General Vasily Chuikov promised him, "We will hold Stalingrad or die there!"

BELOW: Soviet troops defend the city of Stalingrad against German forces in November 1942.

RIVAL GENERALS

CHUIKOV
General Vasily Chuikov (1900–82) was commander of the 62nd Army, holding Stalingrad. He ordered his men to stay as close to the enemy as possible, seeking hand-to-hand combat. This strategy of holding the enemy close meant that German planes and artillery could not attack the Soviet defenders without hitting their own men.

PAULUS
General Friedrich Paulus (1890–1957), commander of the German 6th Army, led the attack on Stalingrad. When defeat seemed inevitable, Hitler made him a field marshal. This promotion put pressure on him to fight to the last man, since no German field marshal had ever surrendered before. Despite this, Paulus disobeyed orders and surrendered.

RAT WARFARE
The Germans bombarded Stalingrad with Stuka dive-bombers and artillery, reducing large areas to rubble. The 6th Army then forced its way into the city, and fierce street battles were fought in the ruins. The Soviets made great use of snipers, trained marksmen who shot at the Germans from concealed positions. They traveled using the sewers, leading the Germans to nickname the battle "Rattenkrieg" (Rat War). Every building was bitterly fought over—the railway station changed hands 15 times in five days. Yet, little by little, the Germans conquered most of the city. In November, Hitler declared, "We have got it! There are only a few places not captured."

SOVIET TRAP

Unknown to Hitler, while the 6th Army was conquering the city, Soviet forces were gathering for a counterattack. On November 19, the Red Army advanced north and south of Stalingrad, encircling the Germans. Field Marshal Paulus asked Hitler for permission to break out before it was too late, but the Führer refused. The 6th Army, with over 250,000 men, was now trapped. For two months they held out, weakened by starvation and cold. On February 2, 1943, Field Marshal Paulus, with only 91,000 German survivors, surrendered.

ОТСТОИМ
ВОЛГУ-МАТУШКУ!

ABOVE LEFT: A Soviet poster shows the defenders of Stalingrad. The slogan "Let's defend the Volga" refers to the city's river.

BELOW: Soldiers of the German 6th Army, fighting in the ruins of Stalingrad in November 1942.

BELOW: German prisoners of war, on their way to Soviet prison camps in 1943.

"Never before in Germany's history have so large a body of troops come to so dreadful an end."

German General Siegfried von Weatphal 1943

KEY SNIPER SKILLS

THE BEST SNIPERS:

• choose where to fire from very carefully: a place where they can hide, but see their surroundings well.

• hide in the shade, because sunlight reflected in the telescopic sights of the rifle can reveal where they are to an enemy.

• wait patiently for just the right moment to shoot at their target.

• find another position after firing one or two shots, because the enemy will have been alerted to their position.

KHARKOV AND KURSK

The German defeat at Stalingrad was a disaster, but Hitler did not give up his dream of conquering the Soviet Union. In 1943, two more great battles were fought at Kharkov and Kursk.

On February 5, 1943, Hitler met Field Marshal Erich von Manstein, commander of his armies in the southern Soviet Union. With his confidence shaken, Hitler said, "I alone bear the responsibility for Stalingrad." Hitler's strategy of refusing to give up captured territory had led to the disaster. Now he allowed Manstein to use a more flexible strategy.

When the Red Army attacked Kharkov in February 1943, Manstein's forces withdrew, giving the impression they were retreating. The Germans waited, in concentrated pockets, for the Soviet troops to overstretch themselves. On February 19, Manstein launched a counterattack. By March 19, Manstein had recaptured Kharkov, restoring the crumbling German front.

"Victory at Kursk will be a beacon for the whole world."

Adolf Hitler, 15 April 1943

LEFT: German soldiers fire on the Soviets in Kharkov during their capture of the city.

THE BATTLE OF KURSK

When Hitler's attack began on July 5, the Soviets were ready for it. They had been warned by spies at German headquarters. In the north, the Germans could only advance 10 miles before they ground to a halt. There was better progress in the south, where the tanks advanced 25 miles, but at a terrible cost. After one week of heavy fighting, Hitler, who had lost half of his 2,700 tanks in the battle, decided to call off the attack. This brought the last German offensive in the east to an end. From that point on, Hitler's armies would be on the retreat.

OPERATION CITADEL

In April 1943, Hitler ordered a new offensive, called Operation Citadel. The target was a bulge in the Soviet front line around the city of Kursk, to the north of Kharkov. To ensure success, Hitler delayed the attack until July, when his army would have new Panther tanks that could outclass the Soviet T-34s. This delay gave the Red Army time to prepare elaborate defenses 200 miles deep. By July, the Kursk bulge held 1.3 million Soviet soldiers, with 20,000 artillery guns, 3,600 tanks, and 2,400 planes.

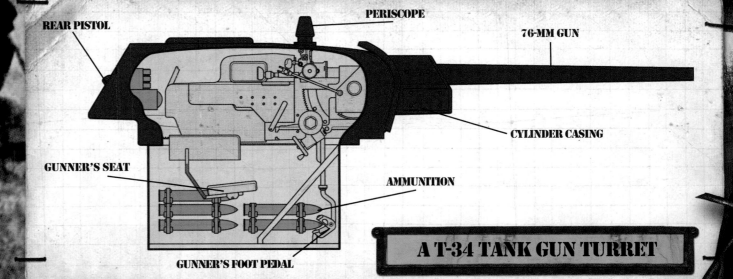

RIGHT: Soviet artillery bombard the Germans at Kharkov. The Soviets recaptured the city one month after the Battle of Kursk.

ABOVE: Soviet tanks, followed by Red Army infantrymen, attack the German forces at Kursk.

REAR PISTOL

PERISCOPE

76-MM GUN

CYLINDER CASING

GUNNER'S SEAT

AMMUNITION

GUNNER'S FOOT PEDAL

A T-34 TANK GUN TURRET

The United States and Soviet Union were the world's leading industrial nations. Unlike Germany and Japan, they had plentiful supplies of raw materials and millions of workers willing to help in the war effort.

With more than seven million people without jobs at the outbreak of the war, it was easy for the United States to find workers. But as more factories were built and men joined the armed forces, the demand for labor grew. Women, teenagers, and the elderly started to work in war factories. A 1942 hit song, "Rosie the Riveter," celebrated the female factory worker, "making history, working for victory."

ABOVE: B-24 Liberator bomber planes being assembled on the production line of a US factory.

LEFT: A US poster encouraging the war effort, showing a female factory worker.

LEFT: To help pay for the war, the US government borrowed money from the public by selling war bonds, a type of savings that people could cash in later.

FACTORY PRODUCTION

The United States was already a world leader in factory production. Unlike Japan and Germany, the country was out of reach of enemy planes, so production was never interrupted by bombing raids.

Manufacturing methods were improved all the time. In 1942, Henry Kaiser's shipyards on the West Coast were able to cut the time taken to build a ship from six months to just four weeks. The United States was building ships faster than Germany and Japan could sink them.

AIRCRAFT PRODUCTION

Rival aircraft companies worked together during wartime. Though designed by Boeing, the B-17 Flying Fortress bomber was also produced in other companies' factories. At their peak, these factories turned out 15 Flying Fortresses a day. In 1944, the United States produced 114,000 combat planes, more than three times as many as Germany.

COMMUNIST PRODUCTION

Unlike other wartime nations, the Soviet Union was a communist society, with no private businesses. All industries and workers were under state control, a system of government that greatly helped the Soviet war effort.

Soon after the German invasion, Stalin moved 1,523 factories east to beyond the Ural Mountains, out of reach of German bombers. Around 25 million workers were sent to run the factories. They were forced to work a 66-hour week. Communist rule had been widely unpopular, so Stalin presented the struggle against Germany as a "Great Patriotic War." The people were called on to defend their land against the Nazi invaders.

ABOVE: A T-34 tank being assembled in a Soviet factory. Some tanks were painted white for winter camouflage.

RUSSIAN TANK FACTORY

During the war, Soviet factories produced 105,251 tanks, compared to 88,410 in the United States and 67,429 in Germany. More than half the Soviet tanks were T-34s. With wide tracks and a powerful engine, the T-34 was faster than early German tanks and had an excellent mix of mobility, firepower, and armor. Even the Germans admired the T-34, which has influenced tank design ever since.

"Their T-34 tank was the finest in the world."
German Field Marshal Paul von Kleist on the Soviet tank

AMERICAN CHILDREN DO THEIR PART

In America in 1944, up to three million young boys and girls worked in factories, shops, and restaurants. Younger children helped the war effort by becoming Junior Commandos. There was a military-style ranking system for Junior Commandos where promotion was earned by different acts, including:

- collecting scrap metal to recycle into guns, ships, tanks, and ammunition
- picking wild milkweed pods to use in sailors' life jackets
- buying war bonds with pocket money to raise funds for the war
- assembling care packages for soldiers at the front

SOVIET WOMEN

Communists thought that women could do the same jobs as men, including hard physical work. Women mined coal, worked on building sites, and ran the railways. As they were paid less than men, they were an ideal source of cheap factory labor. By 1945, women made up 56 percent of the Soviet workforce. About 800,000 women also joined the army, fighting as snipers, machine gunners, tank drivers, and pilots.

BELOW: These Soviet women are putting grease on artillery shells in a war factory.

Deutsche Frauen und Mädel!

Helft mit bei der Reichsbahn!

Wenn das Arbeitsamt Euch ruft:
Meldet Euch bei den Reichsbahn-Dienststellen.

LEFT: German women were not called to work in factories until 1944, but they could serve on the railways. This poster is asking women to help out.

Despite their best efforts, Germany and Japan could not compete with the Allies in industrial production. They lacked fuel and raw materials, and their factories were vulnerable to bombing.

In Germany and Japan, the government controlled the lives of its citizens. Robert Ley, a senior Nazi, wrote, "The only people who still have a private life in Germany are those who are asleep." Similarly, an official Japanese publication declared, "Even in our private lives we should be devoted to the Emperor." Every Japanese civilian was a member of a *tonarigumi* (neighborhood association) whose leader reported on the members' loyalty.

In both countries, it was illegal to voice doubts about the war. In Germany, people who spoke against the Nazis risked arrest by the Gestapo, the feared secret police.

GERMAN FACTORIES

The German economy was not completely directed to the war. Women were not conscripted for factory work, as Hitler believed that their place was in the home. War factories used many foreign workers from conquered lands, and prisoners of war. In 1942, the failure to conquer the Soviet Union meant that Germany needed more tanks and planes. Between 1942 and 1944, the armaments minister, Albert Speer, tripled production, but this would not be enough for victory.

LEFT: Heinkel bombers on the production line in a German war factory.

38

BELOW: Germans force Polish Jews in Warsaw to clear rubble.

RIGHT: In Japanese camps, thousands of Allied prisoners of war died of starvation, disease, and beatings from guards.

SLAVE LABOR

Both Germany and Japan used foreigners as slave labor. Prisoners under both were treated harshly. The Germans had the slave labor of the Jews and other foreigners rounded up and sent to ghettos and concentration camps. The Japanese forced prisoners to build railways or to work in mines and factories.

HITLER YOUTH

NAZI YOUTH GROUP

German boys were expected to be members of the Hitler Youth, the Nazi youth organization. On joining at the age of ten, they had to say, "I swear to devote all my energies to the savior of our country, Adolf Hitler." They were toughened up with countryside hikes; as they marched, they sang songs praising the Nazis. There was also a girls' organization, whose members were taught to be good wives and mothers.

RIGHT: Boys of the Hitler Youth parade in an open-air camp near Berlin.

HOME FRONT IN JAPAN

In Japan's factories, old people, women, and teenagers worked long hours, often all week, to help the war. The government told them that Japan was fighting a just war, started by the Americans. Radios and newspapers never mentioned Japanese defeats. However, life grew harder as food ran short and cities began to be hit by US bomber planes.

ABOVE: This postcard, showing Japanese women working in the fields, was a reminder of home carried by a Japanese soldier.

THE HOLOCAUST

Between 1939 and 1945, at least six million Jews died at the hands of the Nazis. This deliberate attempt to wipe out the Jewish race in Europe is called the Holocaust.

Hitler had always hated Jews, blaming them, without reason, for most of Germany's problems. After taking power, he passed laws depriving Jewish people of their rights. In 1935, they were stripped of German citizenship and forbidden to marry Aryans—the Nazi name for the Germanic race.

With the arrival of war, millions of European Jews found themselves in German-occupied territory. In Nazi-occupied Poland, the Jews were forced to live in separate areas of cities, called ghettos. Starting in December 1939, they were also made to wear armbands or badges sewn onto their clothing to distinguish them from non-Jews.

LEFT: German soldiers round up Jewish families following an uprising in the Warsaw Ghetto, Poland, in April and May 1943.

> **"Each Jew is a sworn enemy of the German people."**
>
> Joseph Goebbels, Nazi propaganda minister, November 1941

RIGHT: Auschwitz was the largest of all the concentration camps. Outside, on the train tracks, you can make out people's discarded personal belongings.

CONCENTRATION CAMPS

After coming to power, the Nazis set up concentration camps in Germany, including Dachau and Buchenwald, where political opponents were locked up. During the war, many Jews were sent to these camps to work as slaves.

Unlike the German camps, those in Nazi-occupied Poland, such as Auschwitz, were built as death camps. On arrival, most of the Jews were sent to the gas chambers. Some of the strongest people were allowed to live, as long as they helped in the killing process. They had to carry the bodies from the gas chambers to ovens, where they were burned.

RIGHT: Two cans of Zyklon B, the poisonous gas used to kill Jews in the death camps.

FINAL SOLUTION

After invading the Soviet Union in June 1941, the Germans introduced a new policy of killing all the Jews they came across. Special units called *Einsatzgruppen* hunted down Jews and shot them. By December, they had killed 500,000 people. The following January, the Nazis drew up a "final solution to the Jewish problem." All over Europe, Jews would be rounded up and sent to death camps to be killed with poisonous gas, as this was more efficient than shooting.

HIDING FROM THE NAZIS

ANNE FRANK

Anne Frank (1929–45) was a German girl whose Jewish family fled to the Netherlands in 1933 to escape Nazi rule. In 1942, the Franks went into hiding in secret rooms in a house in Amsterdam. They hid for two years, until they were caught. During this time, Anne kept a diary, published in 1947 by her father, the only family member to survive. She wrote, "I believe, in spite of everything, that people are truly good at heart."

ABOVE: Anne Frank, photographed in May 1942, two months before her family went into hiding.

SECRET WAR

A great part of World War II took place in secret. This was the deadly world of resistance fighters and spies, who carried out dangerous operations behind enemy lines.

FRENCH RESISTANCE

There was organized resistance to the Germans in all the territories they occupied. In France, resistance fighters distributed anti-German leaflets, helped escaping prisoners of war, and carried out acts of sabotage. This was dangerous work because those captured by the Germans were tortured to reveal the identity of their comrades, then shot.

In 1944, the Allies, planning to invade Europe, were helped by members of the French Resistance, who passed on information about German troop movements. Between April and May 1944, resistance fighters blew up 1,800 railway engines used by the Germans to transport troops and equipment. After the Allied invasion in June, the French Resistance openly fought the Germans as a proper army called the FFI (French Forces of the Interior). By October 1944, the FFI had 400,000 soldiers.

LEFT: A resistance fighter, wearing an identification armband, fights alongside Allied troops, on the way to Paris in 1944.

BELOW: Members of the FFI, in uniform, lead away a captured German soldier.

LEFT: Three Soviet female partisans in civilian clothes. They are armed with rifles fitted with bayonets.

PARTISANS

Civilians who attack an enemy in occupied territory are called partisans. In Italy and the German-occupied areas of the Soviet Union, partisans took to the mountains and forests, where they planned ambushes, raids, and acts of sabotage.

Many partisans were Jews, who welcomed the chance to fight the Nazis. Women played an important role in both partisan movements. In Italy, they carried messages and supplies. In the Soviet Union, women fought alongside the men. Sources claim that by 1943 there were 500,000 partisans fighting behind enemy lines in the Soviet Union.

RIGHT: From a distance, this inflatable Sherman tank looks just like the real thing.

DUMMY TANKS

Both sides used dummy tanks to fool the enemy about the true size and location of their forces. Before the 1944 Allied invasion of Normandy, thousands of dummy tanks were built on the coast of Kent, in southeast England. The plan was to trick the Germans into thinking the invasion would take place in Calais, France. It was a great success. The Germans were convinced, and they kept their strongest forces in the Calais area.

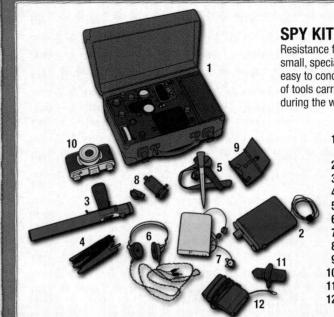

SPY KIT

Resistance fighters and spies needed small, special equipment that was easy to conceal. Here is a selection of tools carried by secret fighters during the war.

1 radio transceiver (to send and receive messages)
2 transmitter
3 silent pistol
4 aerial for transceiver
5 wrist dagger
6 headphones
7 receiver
8 German igniters for booby traps
9 British igniter for booby traps
10 camera to shoot documents
11 adaptor
12 power pack

RICHARD SORGE

The most famous wartime spy was Richard Sorge (1895–1944), a Soviet spy who was half German and half Russian. Beginning in 1933, Sorge lived in Japan, working as a journalist for a German newspaper, pretending to be a Nazi. Sorge passed on many secrets to the Soviet government, but he was eventually caught and hanged.

ABOVE: Sorge's Japanese identity card described him as a journalist for the *Frankfurter Zeitung*, a German newspaper.

ENIGMA MACHINE

The German armed forces sent coded messages created with an Enigma machine. Unknown to them, British intelligence at Bletchley Park in England cracked the Enigma code and read their messages, greatly helping the Allied war effort. This closely guarded secret was revealed in 1974, 29 years after the war ended.

RIGHT: A German Enigma machine converted a message into code. The receiver decoded it using another Enigma machine.

NEW TECH-NOLOGIES

Victory in the war depended as much on scientists as it did on soldiers. On each side, scientists worked hard to develop new weapons and other inventions.

As German defeats mounted, Hitler placed increasing hope for victory on new "secret weapons." In March 1945, he told army officers, "We have invisible aircraft, submarines, colossal tanks and cannon, unbelievably powerful rockets, and a bomb with a working that will astonish the whole world."

One project was the German Messerschmitt-262 Schwalbe (Swallow). It was the world's first jet-powered fighter plane, reaching a speed of over 500 miles per hour. Unfortunately for Hitler, it was produced too late in the war to have much impact.

BELOW: A V1 flying bomb, nicknamed a "doodlebug" by the British.

REVENGE WEAPONS

Some of Hitler's new weapons were called *Vergeltungswaffen* (revenge weapons), because they were used to avenge the bombing of German cities. The first was the V-1 flying bomb, which was sent over southern England. At a preset distance, its engine cut off, and it fell to earth where it exploded. The V-2 rocket was even deadlier. It flew at more than 2,000 miles per hour, which made it impossible to see or shoot down. Around 1,400 V-2s were fired against Britain, before their launch sites were captured by the Allies.

BELOW: The V-2 rocket missile, developed by Wernher von Braun, a brilliant German rocket scientist.

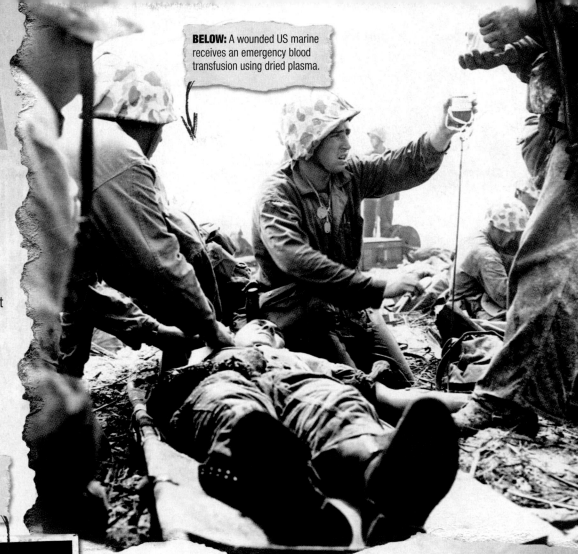

BELOW: A wounded US marine receives an emergency blood transfusion using dried plasma.

PROXIMITY FUZE

One of the greatest Allied inventions was the "proximity fuze"—a radio transmitter and receiver fitted into the nose of a shell. The fuze, in use from January 1943, detected a target and exploded on approaching it. For the first time, enemy planes could be destroyed without a direct hit. The proximity fuze played a major role in defeating the Japanese air force in the Pacific. Although a million people helped make proximity fuzes, the weapon's existence remained secret until after the war.

LEFT: A shell fitted with a proximity fuze. The idea was British in origin but developed in the United States.

BELOW: An atomic bomb explodes in New Mexico, releasing a lethal mushroom cloud of radiated smoke.

ATOMIC BOMB

The most deadly invention of all was the atomic, or nuclear, bomb. In 1938, two German scientists discovered a way of splitting the atom, which, in theory, could release huge amounts of energy. However, some of the best German nuclear scientists were Jews who had fled to the United States to escape the Nazis. Adolf Hitler had no interest in nuclear physics, which he called "Jewish physics." As a result, it was the Allies, not the Germans, who developed the atomic bomb, first tested at Los Alamos, New Mexico, in July 1945.

MEDICINE

There were several medical advances that saved the lives of millions of soldiers and civilians. In 1940, Charles Drew, a US scientist, pioneered a new way to give blood transfusions using dried plasma (the liquid component of blood) mixed with distilled water. Another development was penicillin, a medicine based on a mold that could destroy bacteria. In 1942, a team of scientists in Oxford, England, led by the Australian Howard Florey, found a way to mass-produce the drug. Penicillin was used to treat soldiers whose wounds became infected.

BELOW: Since World War II, penicillin has saved the lives of millions of people.

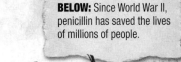

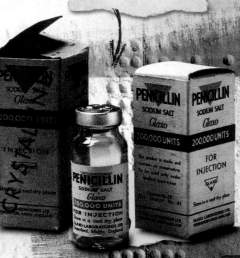

ALLIES IN ITALY

On July 10, 1943, the Allies invaded Sicily, Italy. The invasion force of US, Canadian, and British soldiers met with little resistance from the Italians.

The successful Allied invasion caused a crisis in the Italian leadership. Senior Fascists, together with King Victor Emmanuel III, overthrew Mussolini, placing him under arrest. A new Italian government led by Marshal Pietro Badoglio began to negotiate with the Allies, signing a peace treaty on September 3.

On the same day, the Allies landed at Salerno, in southern Italy. Hitler was furious. While Badoglio and the king fled south to join the Allies, German troops seized control of Rome and the northern two-thirds of the country.

ABOVE: US paratroopers jumping from their planes over Sicily on July 10, 1943.

BATTLE AT ANZIO

The Germans, commanded by Field Marshal Albert Kesselring, put up much tougher resistance than the Italians. South of Rome, Kesselring set up strong defensive lines, running from sea to sea, which slowed the Allied advance. On January 22, 1944, US forces landed at Anzio, north of the German defense lines. This landing came as a big surprise to Kesselring, but he rushed troops into the area and a fierce battle began.

BELOW: US antitank gunners fighting in Anzio, a battle that lasted for more than four months.

ALLIED INVASION IN ITALY
1943–1945

FRANCE
Lyons
SWITZ.
AUSTRIA
Turin
Trieste
Genoa
CROATIA
Marseilles
YUGOSLAVIA
SPAIN
SERBIA
Corsica
ITALY
Rome
Sardinia
Anzio
Monte Cassino
ALBANIA
BULGARIA
Naples
Taranto
Cagliari
Salerno
Mediterranean Sea
Palermo
GREECE
Algiers
Messina
Tunis
Sicily
ALGERIA
TUNISIA

RIGHT: A German antitank "teller mine," used in Italy. When a tank drove over it, the pressure set off an explosion.

TIGER TANK

- MUZZLE BREAK
- 88-MM GUN
- COMMANDER'S HATCH
- MAIN TURRET
- ENGINE ROOM
- MACHINE GUN
- TRACK IDLER
- CATERPILLAR TRACK
- ROAD WHEEL
- DRIVE SPROCKET

ABOVE: The monastery of Monte Cassino, founded in the sixth century, was destroyed by bombing, then later rebuilt.

MONTE CASSINO

With the US troops struggling to break out of Anzio, the Allies began an attack on Monte Cassino, part of the main German defensive line. On February 15, an Allied bombing raid destroyed Monte Cassino's medieval hilltop monastery. The Germans moved into the rubble and held off attacks until May. They were reinforced by armored divisions sent by Kesselring.

The Allied side in the battle consisted of soldiers of many nationalities, including Indians, Gurkhas, Poles, New Zealanders, South Africans, and Frenchmen. The monastery was finally captured on May 18 by Poles, who lost 4,000 men in the assault. A few days later, the Allies in Anzio finally broke through the German defenses. The Germans were now in full retreat.

LEFT: A crowd of Italians in Rome jubilantly celebrate their liberation by the Allies.

LIBERATION OF ROME

After the victories of May 1944, the Allies swept north toward Rome, which was just 33 miles from Anzio. Kesselring, who did not want Italy's ancient capital to be damaged in a battle, withdrew from the city. On June 4, US troops entered Rome and were warmly welcomed by the population. But this was not the end of the Italian campaign—the Germans in northern Italy, with their formidable Tiger tanks, fought on for almost a year. Behind their lines, Italian resistance fighters also fought against the Germans.

MUSSOLINI ESCAPES

A DARING RAID

Two months after his arrest, Mussolini was rescued by the Germans, who discovered he was being held at a ski resort in the Appenine Mountains. On September 12, 1943, 90 German paratroopers led by Colonel Otto Skorzeny stormed the resort. Hitler made Mussolini leader of a short-lived Fascist state in northern Italy. Then, in April 1945, with defeat looming, Mussolini fled and was shot by Italian partisans.

RIGHT: Mussolini is flown to freedom by the Germans in a light airplane called a Fieseler Storch.

ISLAND CAMPAIGN

Following their victory over the Japanese navy at Midway, the United States went on the attack. They began, in August 1942, by invading Guadalcanal, a steamy tropical island northeast of Australia.

BELOW: An American soldier keeping a lookout for Japanese in Guadalcanal in January 1943.

On August 6, 1942, 11,000 US Marines landed at Guadalcanal, beginning six months of hard fighting. The Marines had to learn to fight in the jungle, where it was hard to see the enemy. The Japanese were more experienced jungle fighters, often attacking at night. Despite a lack of Navy support, the Marines, later reinforced by Army units, held off constant enemy assaults. The Japanese had run out of food and medicine by January 1943. In February, the Japanese finally withdrew.

BELOW: US marines landing on the beach at Guadalcanal, with the jungle directly in front of them.

ABOVE: US soldiers used deadly portable flamethrowers for the first time at Guadalcanal.

TOWARD THE PHILIPPINES

From late 1943, the US Pacific Fleet, commanded by Admiral Chester Nimitz, advanced through the western Pacific, capturing one island group after another. All were fiercely defended by Japanese troops, willing to fight to the last man.

Meanwhile, General Douglas MacArthur led an Allied Australian and US army up the coast of New Guinea toward the Philippines. In October 1944, Nimitz and MacArthur came together, in a joint invasion of these islands. MacArthur, who was in the Philippines when the Japanese conquered them, had famously promised to return. On October 20, he landed on the Philippine island of Leyte.

BATTLE OF LEYTE GULF

To defend the Philippines, the Japanese gathered all their ships into one last great fleet. From October 23 to 26, the rival fleets met in the largest sea battle in history, in Leyte Gulf, off the Philippines. It was an overwhelming victory for the Americans, whose bombers sank 24 Japanese ships, including all their aircraft carriers. The Japanese navy was virtually finished.

ABOVE: The US aircraft carrier *Princeton* on fire in Leyte Gulf. This was one of the few American ships lost in the battle.

- Move silently through the dense undergrowth. Any sound can give your location away.

- Speak as little as possible; communicate with one another by hand signals.

- Stay alert at all times, listening for the sounds made by enemy troops.

- Cut down leaves to make camouflage to wear on your clothing, to help you blend in with your surroundings.

"People of the Philippines, I have returned!"

General Douglas MacArthur, October 1944

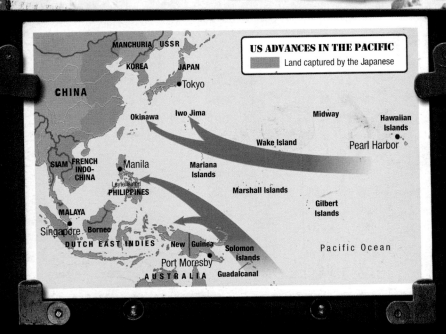

BELOW: General Douglas MacArthur wades ashore at Leyte, in the Philippines, on October 20, 1944

US ADVANCES IN THE PACIFIC
Land captured by the Japanese

MANCHURIA — USSR
KOREA — JAPAN
CHINA
Tokyo
Okinawa — Iwo Jima — Midway — Hawaiian Islands
Wake Island — Pearl Harbor
Manila — Mariana Islands
SIAM — FRENCH INDO-CHINA
Leyte Island — PHILIPPINES — Marshall Islands
MALAYA — Gilbert Islands
Singapore — Borneo
DUTCH EAST INDIES — New Guinea — Solomon Islands — Pacific Ocean
Port Moresby — Guadalcanal
AUSTRALIA

ASSAULT ON JAPAN

By October 1944, the Japanese knew that the war was lost and that Japan would soon be invaded. The Japanese generals were unable to bear the shame of surrender, and resistance became even more desperate.

By late 1944, the best Japanese pilots had all been shot down and the country had little fuel left. The remaining pilots, young men with little training, had no chance of sinking ships by bombing. Instead, the generals asked them to fly planes packed with explosives straight into the decks of the enemy ships.

Almost 3,000 young men volunteered for these suicide missions. They sank about 50 US ships, yet this was not enough to save Japan.

ABOVE: A Zero-Sen fighter plane, the standard model flown by kamikaze pilots.

RIGHT: A young kamikaze pilot ties on his *hachimaki* headband before flying on his doomed mission.

KAMIKAZE HEADBANDS

闘 ● 魂

闘 ● 魂

DEPARTURE RITUAL

Kamikaze pilots wore white headbands called *hachimaki*, or "helmet scarves." They put them on as part of a departure ritual. The bands were decorated with inspirational symbols such as the rising sun (below), the symbol of Japan, or a slogan such as "Fighting Spirit" (above). Still worn in Japan today, these headbands have long denoted commitment in Japanese culture; they signify the wearer's perseverance or effort.

KAMIKAZE

Pilots who flew suicide missions were called kamikaze ("divine winds"), in memory of great storms that had saved Japan from invasion fleets in the 13th century. Kamikaze pilots were told it was an honor to die for their Emperor. One pilot, Isao Matsuo, wrote a farewell letter to his parents in which he said, "Beloved parents. Please congratulate me. I have been given a splendid opportunity to die."

IWO JIMA

The first territory of the Japanese homeland to be invaded was Iwo Jima, a tiny island 600 miles south of Tokyo, where US Marines landed in February 1945. Iwo Jima was fiercely defended by 25,000 Japanese soldiers, who had built a network of tunnels and fortifications. It took over five weeks to capture; 6,825 Americans died and more than 20,000 were wounded. Almost all the Japanese died, with only 1,083 taken prisoner.

BELOW: Marines on Iwo Jima take shelter as they blow up the entrance to a cave used by Japanese defenders.

FIRE RAIDS ON JAPAN

Meanwhile, US bomber planes attacked the Japanese home islands, dropping firebombs on the cities, whose wooden buildings quickly caught fire. By now there was almost no resistance from the Japanese air force. A huge raid took place on March 9, 1945, when 279 bombers attacked Tokyo. In a great firestorm that swept the city, between 90,000 and 100,000 civilians were burned to death. A survivor recalled, "I watched hundreds of people, adults and children, running for their lives, dashing madly about like rats."

LEFT: US Navy carrier-based aircraft flying over Tokyo in March 1945.

BELOW: The ruins of Tokyo, photographed from a US plane, in September 1945.

"The gods would weep at the bravery of my officers and men."

General Kuribayashi, Japanese commander in Iwo Jima

D-DAY

While war raged in the Soviet Union and the Pacific, the Allies were planning to liberate western Europe from the Nazis. A massive invasion force was being built in Britain, ready for landings on the Normandy coast of France.

The planning for Operation Overlord, as the D-Day landings were officially known, began in 1943. The aim for the first 24 hours was to establish a beachhead—an area of land that could be defended against enemy attack. The Allied leaders chose American General Eisenhower as supreme commander of the operation, while British General Montgomery led the ground troops.

LEFT: An American soldier moves along Utah Beach on D-Day.

BELOW: This Bible—carried in an Allied soldier's breast pocket —saved its owner's life when it stopped a German bullet.

RIGHT: German soldiers in a concrete bunker guard the Normandy beaches.

ALLIED COMMANDERS

EISENHOWER

Dwight D. Eisenhower, or "Ike" as he was known, was Supreme Allied Commander. He commanded British, Canadian, American, and French troops, and it was essential that they cooperated well. After the war, Eisenhower remained in the army until 1952. He was elected president of the United States later that year and took office in 1953.

MONTGOMERY

Bernard Law Montgomery was known as "Monty." In 1942, he won the crucial Battle of El Alamein in North Africa, and the following year he led the British invasions of Sicily and southern Italy.

NORMANDY LANDINGS

Eisenhower planned to get round 100,000 men—plus tanks, guns, and equipment—ashore in the first 24 hours. Normandy was the only stretch of the French coast with wide enough beaches. D-Day began just after midnight on June 6, 1944, as paratroops floated from the skies to seize bridges and road junctions. At dawn, over 600 warships and 3,000 transport ships arrived off the Normandy coast. The warships opened fire on the German defenses and then men began wading ashore.

STORMING THE BEACHES

The Normandy coast was divided into five landing areas. In the east was Sword Beach, where the British were to land; then came Juno Beach for the Canadians, Gold Beach for the British, Omaha Beach for the Americans, and Utah Beach in the west, another American landing area. The infantry, landing from special shallow-draft craft, were supported by tanks equipped with special canvas floats to enable them to "swim" ashore.

Although the fighting was savage, the landings went well in most areas. At Omaha Beach, however, the German defenses were stronger than expected. The US 1st Division was pinned down by machine-gun fire and took heavy casualties. By dusk they had gotten off the beach but had failed to link up with the other landing forces.

"You are about to embark on the great crusade toward which we have striven these many months. The eyes of the world are upon you."

Eisenhower's message to Allied troops before D-Day

TANK ATTACK

By midnight on D-Day, only 132,000 men were on land, fewer than Eisenhower had wanted. The city of Caen was still in German hands—as was the town of Carentan. The Germans were bringing up reinforcements, including the 21st Panzer Division from Caen, and attacking British positions. The Allies had a foothold in France, but there was still much fighting to be done.

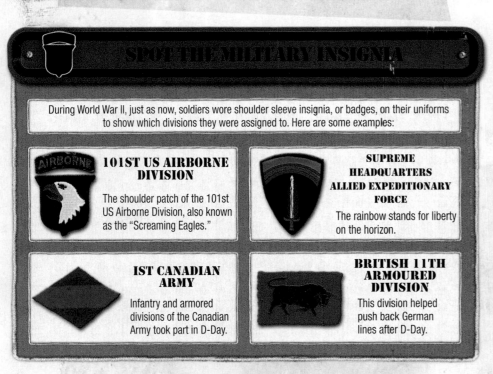

SPOT THE MILITARY INSIGNIA

During World War II, just as now, soldiers wore shoulder sleeve insignia, or badges, on their uniforms to show which divisions they were assigned to. Here are some examples:

101ST US AIRBORNE DIVISION

The shoulder patch of the 101st US Airborne Division, also known as the "Screaming Eagles."

SUPREME HEADQUARTERS ALLIED EXPEDITIONARY FORCE

The rainbow stands for liberty on the horizon.

1ST CANADIAN ARMY

Infantry and armored divisions of the Canadian Army took part in D-Day.

BRITISH 11TH ARMOURED DIVISION

This division helped push back German lines after D-Day.

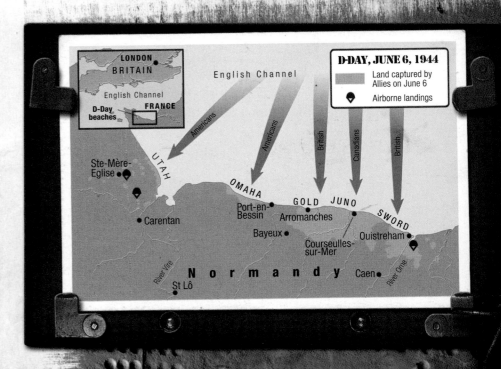

D-DAY, JUNE 6, 1944

Land captured by Allies on June 6

Airborne landings

LONDON BRITAIN

English Channel

English Channel

D-Day beaches

FRANCE

Americans

Americans

British

Canadians

British

Ste-Mère-Eglise

UTAH

OMAHA

GOLD

JUNO

SWORD

Port-en-Bessin

Arromanches

Courseulles-sur-Mer

Ouistreham

Carentan

Bayeux

River Vire

St Lô

Normandy

Caen

River Orne

GERMANY RETREATS

Following the D-Day landings, the western Allies advanced through France, winning battle after battle. In the east, the Soviet Red Army was also advancing. Everywhere, the Germans were in retreat.

In most countries, the Allies were welcomed as liberators. It was a different matter in Poland. Many Poles hated and feared the Soviets, who had invaded their country in 1920 and in 1939. There was bitter rivalry between the democratic Polish government-in-exile, based in London, and a provisional government of Polish Communists, formed by Stalin in July 1944. Stalin did not want the democratic government to take power after the war.

WARSAW UPRISING

On August 1, 1944, the government-in-exile ordered an uprising in the capital, Warsaw, by the Polish resistance. The aim was to liberate the city before the approaching Red Army got there. The uprising lasted for two months, until it was finally crushed by the Germans. The Red Army, on the banks of the Vistula River just a few miles away, did nothing to help.

BELOW: Soldiers of the Polish Home Army, fighting from barricades in Warsaw. Around 15,000 soldiers and 200,000 civilians were killed.

BELOW: A US Sherman tank driven by the Free French army passes the Arc de Triomphe in Paris in August 1944.

LIBERATION OF PARIS

A more successful uprising was staged by the French Resistance in Paris on August 19. Although 17,000 German troops occupied major buildings, they did little to suppress the uprising. Hitler ordered the German governor of Paris, General von Choltitz, to destroy the capital, saying, "The city must not fall into the enemy's hand except lying in complete debris." Choltitz, horrified at the destruction of a beautiful city, disobeyed Hitler's order. On August 23, US and French troops entered Paris to find streets filled with celebrating Parisians. Two days later, Choltitz surrendered.

BELOW: On August 25, General Charles de Gaulle, leader of the Free French, reentered Paris in triumph.

By 1943, many senior German army officers believed the war was lost. A group plotted to kill Hitler, overthrow the Nazi regime, and make peace with the Allies. In July 1944, the plotters exploded a bomb, hidden in a briefcase, at Hitler's headquarters. Hitler survived, with minor injuries, and crushed the conspiracy. Among 4,980 people executed for being part of the plot, there were 18 generals.

LEFT: The remains of the Nazi headquarters where the bomb exploded.

LEFT: During the Battle of the Bulge, German troops in Belgium head toward Malmedy, where the Germans murdered 90 US prisoners of war.

INSIDE A SHERMAN

MACHINE GUN

75-MM GUN

COMMANDER'S HATCH

GUNNER'S SEAT

75-MM ROUNDS

CATERPILLAR TRACK

CHRYSLER ENGINE

TRACK IDLER

BATTLE OF THE BULGE

In December 1944, Hitler ordered a last, desperate offensive, in the Ardennes. To gather enough troops, old men and teenage boys were mobilized. The attack was a complete surprise to the Allies, and the Germans made an initial breakthrough. Yet the Battle of the Bulge was doomed to fail through lack of fuel and ammunition. By the end, on January 25, there were 75,000 US and 100,000 German casualties. When the Soviets began their next eastern offensive, in January 1945, the German army had no reserves to resist with.

GERMANY DEFEATED

By the beginning of 1945, Allied armies were on the eastern and western borders of Germany, ready to invade. One key target was the capital, Berlin, where Hitler had his headquarters.

In January 1945, the Red Army began a new offensive in the east. The German forces, short of fuel and ammunition, were easily defeated. Millions of civilians fled west, terrified that the Soviet soldiers would take revenge for the German invasion of the Soviet Union. By the end of January, the Red Army had reached the River Oder, just 60 miles from Berlin.

For the final assault, Stalin gathered a huge force of 2.5 million soldiers, 7,500 aircraft, 41,600 artillery guns, and 6,200 tanks. He wanted to seize Berlin before the western Allies in order to impose Soviet control on as much of Germany as possible.

The Supreme Allied Commander, General Eisenhower, left the German capital to the Soviets. He knew the battle for Berlin would cost vast numbers of lives.

ABOVE: By March 1945, the German city of Cologne, bombed 462 times by the Allies, lay in ruins. Despite 14 hits, Cologne cathedral still stood.

BELOW: On May 2, Meliton Kantaria, a Soviet soldier, raised the Red flag on the Reichstag in Berlin.

LEFT: Soviet artillery and tanks pound buildings in Berlin as they advance into the city.

ALLIED ADVANCE ON GERMANY
May 1945

BELOW: A room in the *Führerbunker* (leader's shelter) photographed by the Soviets after 2 May 1945, when they captured it from the Germans.

IN THE *FÜHRERBUNKER*

On January 16, Adolf Hitler moved into an underground bunker in Berlin, where he spent the last three months of his life. From there, he issued orders for counterattacks, which had no chance of taking place. He told Albert Speer, the head of armaments production, to destroy the country's factories and power companies so they would not fall into enemy hands. Speer protested that this would make life impossible for the German people. Hitler replied, "If the war is lost, the German people will also perish." On April 30, as the Red Army fought toward his bunker, Hitler shot himself. By May 8, the war in Europe was over.

LEFT: On April 25, 1945, advancing Soviet and US troops met for the first time at the River Elbe in Germany, and shook hands.

> **"I choose to die rather than bear the shame of overthrow or surrender."**
>
> Adolf Hitler, Last Will, April 29, 1945

DEFENDING BERLIN

From late April, the Red Army fought its way into Berlin from all directions. The city was defended by 90,000 German soldiers. Half were old men and teenagers belonging to the Volkssturm ("People's Storm"), the German home guard formed in September 1944.

Although they were outnumbered, the German soldiers held strong defensive positions in the ruins of Berlin. Armed with handheld antitank weapons called *Panzerfäuste* ("tank fists"), the Germans destroyed 2,000 Soviet tanks. By the end, about 70,000 Soviet soldiers had been killed in the fierce street fighting. More than twice as many Germans died.

CHILDREN OF THE NAZI REGIME

BOY SOLDIERS

Members of the Hitler Youth also fought in the battle. About 5,000 defended bridges over the Havel River, on the west side of Berlin. Many were just 12 years old, and wore steel helmets too big for their heads. Within five days, 4,500 had been killed or wounded. On his 56th birthday, on April 20, 1945, Hitler made his last public appearance, awarding medals to some of these boy soldiers.

LEFT: Hitler gives Iron Cross medals to boys of the Hitler Youth in the garden of the Reich Chancellery on March 20, 1945.

ATOMIC BOMB

BELOW: A deadly mushroom cloud rises over the city of Hiroshima in Japan in 1945.

On April 12, 1945, President Roosevelt died suddenly and was replaced by his vice president, Harry S Truman. Truman learned that the United States had a terrible secret weapon, the atomic bomb.

By now, it was clear that Japan had lost the war, but the Japanese continued to resist. On April 1, US troops had invaded Okinawa, to the southwest of Japan. The battle cost the lives of 12,613 Americans and 110,000 Japanese and Okinawans. Truman was advised that invading Japan itself could lead to the deaths of one million Americans. The president saw the atomic bomb as a way to end the war quickly, saving American lives.

ABOVE: After taking office as president, Harry S Truman said to reporters, "Boys, if you ever pray, pray for me now!"

LEFT: The atomic bomb was first tested at Alamogordo in New Mexico in July 1945. Here, US workers prepare for the test.

ENOLA GAY

THE ATOMIC BOMB IS DROPPED

In August 1945, the United States had just two atomic bombs. Truman decided to use them, without warning, to shock the Japanese into surrendering. The first target was Hiroshima, one of the few cities not already devastated by US bombing raids. On August 6, 1945, Lieutenant Colonel Paul Tibbets flew over Hiroshima in a B-29 bomber and dropped the first bomb, nicknamed "Little Boy." It created a huge mushroom cloud and destroyed most of the city, killing more than 66,000 civilians, most of whom died in the immediate aftermath of the blast.

LEFT: Lieutenant Colonel Paul Tibbets stands in front of his bomber plane. It was named *Enola Gay*, after his mother.

LEFT: This bottle was melted in the intense heat of the Hiroshima blast.

BELOW: The devastation caused by the second atomic bomb at Nagasaki. This area, where houses used to stand, is two miles from where the bomb exploded.

NAGASAKI

On August 9, the United States dropped the second bomb, nicknamed "Fat Man," on Nagasaki, killing 40,000 people. Thousands more would die later from wounds and a new disease called radiation sickness. For days, Japanese leaders, fearing the Americans would depose their emperor, argued over whether to surrender. Finally, on August 14, Emperor Hirohito summoned his aides and said, "I cannot let my subjects suffer any longer." The following day he announced Japan's surrender in the first radio broadcast made by a Japanese emperor. With great understatement, Hirohito declared, "The war situation has developed not necessarily to Japan's advantage." Across the nation, millions of people listened and wept.

END OF THE WAR

The world was very different in 1945 than in 1939, when the war started. The war had created two superpowers, the United States and the Soviet Union, who would now compete to influence the world.

From 1945 to 1951, Japan was occupied by the Allied powers, commanded by General Douglas MacArthur. With a team of legal experts, MacArthur drew up new rules of government to remake Japan a US-style democracy.

The people were given the right to elect their leaders, and new political parties were formed. The emperor, allowed to stay on as a figurehead, was no longer to be thought of as divine. The constitution declared that Japan had given up warfare forever and would no longer have any armed forces.

LEFT: General Yoshijuro Umezu signs the Japanese surrender document, watched by General MacArthur (left).

"We, the Japanese people, desire peace for all time."
1946 Constitution of Japan

VICTORY CELEBRATIONS

The winning nations all held victory celebrations. The German surrender on V-E (Victory in Europe) Day was celebrated on May 8 by the western Allies and the following day in the Soviet Union. In cities such as London and New York, everybody took to the streets. They danced, waved flags, and burned models of Hitler on bonfires.

After the Japanese surrender in August, there were even bigger street celebrations in America. Speaking to a crowd on V-J (Victory over Japan) Day, on August 15, President Truman said, "This is the day we have been waiting for since Pearl Harbor. This is the day when Fascism finally dies, as we always knew it would."

LEFT: Children at a London street party in July 1945, celebrating the end of the war in Europe.

RIGHT: People partying in Times Square, New York, to celebrate the end of of the war in Europe in May 1945.

GERMANY DIVIDED

After the war, the German economy lay in ruins. German cities had been reduced to rubble, and millions were homeless. The country was divided in two, with the west becoming the Federal Republic of Germany, a democratic state allied with the United States and Britain. To the east stood the German Democratic Republic, a Communist state dominated by Stalin. The capital, Berlin, located in the German Democratic Republic, was divided between east and west by a concrete barrier known as the Berlin Wall. From 1948 to 1951, the United States spent 1.448 billion dollars rebuilding the West German economy to create a strong state able to withstand Soviet influence. Germany now stood on the front line of a Cold War between the superpowers. It would remain divided until the collapse of Communism in 1990.

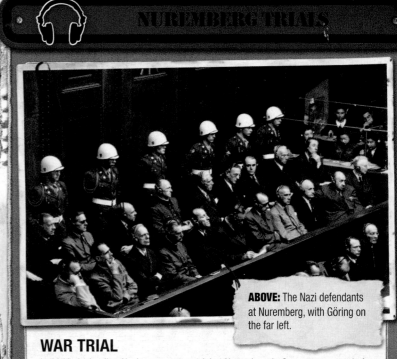

ABOVE: The Nazi defendants at Nuremberg, with Göring on the far left.

WAR TRIAL

In 1946, 21 leading Nazis were put on trial at Nuremberg in Germany, accused of war crimes. A new set of international laws was created, in which murder and other inhumane acts against civilians were called "crimes against humanity." The leading defendant, Hermann Göring, described this as unfair victors' justice. He said, "The victor will always be the judge and the vanquished the accused." Condemned to death by hanging, Göring took poison in his cell before the sentence could be carried out. There were several other trials, including that of the Japanese leader General Tojo, who was hanged.

ABOVE: German children lining up for soup in 1946. Many had lived most of their lives in wartime.

GLOSSARY AND INDEX

ARTILLERY: Guns used in fighting on land that fire missiles called shells.

COMMONWEALTH: Association of nations, such as Canada and Australia, that once made up the British Empire.

COMMUNISM: A system of government based on common ownership of property and industry, aimed at creating a classless society.

CONVOY: A group of merchant ships accompanied by warships for protection.

COUNTER-ATTACK: An attack by a defending force in reply to an attack by the enemy.

DEMOCRACY: Government by the people. In modern democracies, the people choose their rulers in elections.

DICTATOR: A ruler who assumes absolute power.

FASCISM: A political movement that is led by a dictator, believes that the nation is more important than the individual, and suppresses opposition through terror.

FRONT / FRONT LINE: The foremost line of an army fighting the enemy, or the scene of fighting.

GOVERNMENT-IN-EXILE: A government forced to move to a friendly country when its homeland is invaded and occupied by an enemy.

INDEPENDENCE: Freedom from control or influence.

INFANTRY: A body of soldiers trained to fight on foot.

OFFENSIVE: A term for a military campaign or attack.

RESISTANCE: A secret organization fighting the occupying enemy forces in a conquered country.

SOVIET UNION: The nations, including Russia, that formed the Union of Soviet Socialist Republics (1922–1991). Also known as the USSR.

STRATEGY: An overall plan of action for a military force.

PICTURE CREDITS

The majority of photographs reproduced in the book have been taken from the collection of the **Imperial War Museum**. The Museum's reference numbers for each of their photographs are listed below, giving the page on which they appear in the book, and any location indicator.

Key: t – top, b – bottom, c – centre, l – left and r – right

7 (tl) HU 3491, 8-9 (c) MH 11040, 11 (br) D 2239, 14 (tr) PST 13850, 15 (tr) PST 8105, 15 (bc) PST 0059, 17 (tl) HU 41240, 17 (bc) HU 3266, 17 (tr) MUN 3286, 18 (tl badge) INS 7997, 18 (bl) CH 1398, 18 (br New Zealand) INS 7991, 18 (br Canada) INS 7993, 18 (br Rhodesia) INS 8012 19 (tl) CH 3517, 19 (bc) CH 15188, 19 (bl) COL 188, 20 (bl) C 5422, 20-21 (c) H 5593 colour has been added to the Imperial War Museum original image, 21 (tr) HU 44272, 26 (tr) HU 5625, 29 (tr) NYP 68079, 43 (tc) H 42531, 46 (bc) MUN 3314, 47 (tr) MH 11250, 52 (cr) TR 1042, 55 (tr) MH 2111 B, 55 (cr) EA 47958, 59 (tl) HU 44878, 60 (bl) A 30427, 61 (tr) MH 24088
All other items photographed at the Imperial War Museum.

Photographs reproduced from sources outside the Imperial War Museum, with kind permission of:
AKG-Images: 16 (br). 26 (br), 35 (r), 38 (l), 39 (tl); /RIA Novosti: 32 (c), 33 (tl); /Michael Teller: 41 (bc); /Ullstein Bild: 6 (tr), 34 (bl), 56 (r)
Alamy: Daniel Templeton: 11 (bc)
Corbis: 7 (br), 10, 16 (tr), 21 (c), 30 (br), 42 (bc), 45 (tr), 47 (br), 48 (bc), 55 (tl), 58 (r); /Bettmann: 9 (tc), 13 (tl), 18 (tr), 23 (tl), 29 (c), 36 (tr), 38 (bc), 46 (br), 56 (tr), 57 (cl), 61 (br); /Hulton-Deutsch Collection: 6 (bl), 11 (cl), 39 (bl), 47 (cl), 54 (r); /Michael Nicholson: 9 (tr); /Swim Ink 2, LLC: 36 (br); /Underwood & Underwood: 9 (br)
Getty Images: 12 (l), 14 (bl), 14 (br), 15 (br), 19 (tr), 21 (br), 23 (c), 23 (bc), 32 (bl), 35 (tl), 36 (bl), 37 (br), 37 (cl), 41 (br), 41 (tr), 45 (bc), 46 (c), 49 (tr), 50 (r), 58 (tc); /AFP: 13 (tr), 27 (bc), 54 (bl); /Science & Society Picture Library: 45 (br); /Time & Life Pictures: 22 (tr), 45 (tl), 57 (tr), 57 (br), 58 (bl), 59 (br), 61 (c); /Roger Viollet: 40 (bl)
National Archives, Washington D.C.: 6 (cr), 28 (bl), 29 (br), 30 (tl), 30 (bl), 31 (tr), 48 (tr), 49 (br), 51 (l), 52 (tc)
Photos12.com: Ann Ronan: 40-41, 42 (c)
Press Association Images: AP Photo: 22 (br), 33 (tr), 48 (bl), 51 (cr), 51 (br), 52 (bl), 53 (tl); /DPA: 42-43
Private Collection: 39 (bc), 43 (cr), 50 (c), 52 (br)
Science & Society Picture Library: 43 (bc)
Topfoto.co.uk: 33, 39 (tr); /RIA Novosti: 34 (br), 56 (bl); /Roger-Viollet: 23 (tr); /Ullstein Bild: 10 (bl), 26 (bl), 32 (cr), 33 (br), 44 (c), 44 (bc)

Every effort has been made to acknowledge correctly and contact the source and/or copyright holder of each picture, item of memorabilia and artwork, and Carlton Publishing Group apologizes for any unintentional errors, or omissions, which will be corrected in future editions of this book.

Map illustrations by Martin Brown.